Feet In L.A.,
But My Womb Lives In Jerusalem,
My Breath In Vermont

Lori Levy

Teaneck, New Jersey

FEET IN L.A., BUT MY WOMB LIVES IN JERUSALEM, MY BREATH IN
VERMONT ©2023 Lori Levy. All rights reserved. No part of this book may
be used or reproduced in any manner whatsoever without written permission
except in the case of brief quotations embodied in critical articles and reviews.

Published by Ben Yehuda Press
122 Ayers Court #1B
Teaneck, NJ 07666

http://www.BenYehudaPress.com

To subscribe to our monthly book club and support independent Jewish
publishing, visit https://www.patreon.com/BenYehudaPress

Jewish Poetry Project #38   http://jpoetry.us

Ben Yehuda Press books may be purchased at a discount by synagogues, book
clubs, and other institutions buying in bulk. For information, please email
markets@BenYehudaPress.com

Cover illustration: Acrylic painting on canvas of Nahal Yavnael in northern
Israel by Katie Brayer.

ISBN13 978-1-953829-58-0

23 24 25 / 10 9 8 7 6 5 4 3 2 1   20231010

For Avi, with love.

Contents

Where Is Home?	1
Once	2
Roots	4
Tradition	6
Ritual	7
Spice	8
Craving	9
Burgers and Prayers	10
Love in The Time Of Alzheimer's	11
Black Eyes	13
Five Minutes	15
In a Ziploc	16
Survival	17
On Doing Nothing	18
Sweet Tea	19
Four Women Floating	20
Breakfast On The Balcony	21
I Fly To Israel For My Mother's 84th Birthday	22
Sparks	23
In Israel, Tasting Kumquats	24
Upon Returning From a Trip to Israel	25
Do We Call This a Family?	26
Torah in The Fields	27
Yes, But—	28
When I'm Old and Demented	29
Acknowledgments	30
About the Author	32

WHERE IS HOME?

I belong to the movers, the ones who don't stay put.
We have dug up our roots and planted them elsewhere
again, and again. A question clings to me,
like a toddler at my sleeve, pulling for an answer;
the asking never stops.

I could give you my address, point to a house
behind a gate on a boulevard in Los Angeles.
But sometimes only my feet live here;
the top of me leans from a third-floor balcony
for a glimpse of sea past clotheslines and geraniums,
heart beating to the screech of Tel Aviv.

Or maybe I should say
one foot lives here, *the other* over there;
I straddle the earth, legs spread wide. Some days
I click my heels together and land in Vermont,
ground of my childhood.

My breath lives in Vermont: steam in the air
on a cold winter day. My back is there,
imprinted in the snow, arms making wings.
But my womb is in Jerusalem, where my kids were born,
and my vagina resides here, with my husband in L.A.
I swirl olive oil on a plate of hummus.
It tastes like Mordechai Ben Hillel Street, corner of King George.
I spread some on pita for my hungry grandson,
and *home* becomes the reaching between big hands and
little hands this moment, this day.

ONCE

Once you were an olive tree
twisting love out of
the hard, bony hills of Jerusalem.

Once you were this land I love,
and your blood flowed down
the alleys of this ancient city,
bursting through the cracks in her walls.

Once your soul shone out of your black eyes,
plaintive as the soul of Middle Eastern whines
sung on lips like yours
that have known the taste of sour soup
and kubeh on Friday afternoons;
once when your mother bent
a kerchiefed head over her pots,
a reckless sun jumped in behind her back
and chased away the ghosts of death and war
that floated above your newspaper,
then danced for you on the cold kitchen floor.

Once you held me on a Jerusalem balcony,
and together we looked out on a world
of pines bending under the weight of stories
as long and troubled as
the heart-wrenching moan of the muezzin.

Once we followed the setting sun
and read our future
in the waters of the Mediterranean.

Now you find your visions on another shore,
and when your call comes to me—
like a song in the beaks
of migrating birds—
I remember the days
when I didn't have to choose
between your arms
and the tender, open arms of the olive tree.

ROOTS

It's all in the roots—
how he liked the quiet in my family,
I liked the noise in his.
How, twenty-five years later, the balance shifts,
and as I take turns with my sisters-in-law,
hosting his family for the Sabbath meal,
I think of myself on the back seat of a school bus,
bouncing past cows and manure, red barns, hay—
while he returns to the smells in his mother's kitchen,
to fried meat stuffed into hand-made kubeh,
simmering with celery and turnips in sour green soup.
How it's challah bread and blessings, Friday nights in Los Angeles,
silver and china on white linens.
How he thrives at the head of two long tables
as I carry in platters of chicken and roast,
losing sight of myself in the fever of the room.
How more and more now, when Friday comes,
I yearn for that yard that rolled into woods,
where there was just one playmate across the street
and the next nearest neighbors were up the hill.
How more and more, amid the clamor,
he goes back to the bustle of seven siblings
and a door swinging open all hours of the day;
a boy in a city of stone walls
and arms hanging laundry from its balconies.
How he tastes Jerusalem in the silver wine glass
and I taste Vermont, a blade of grass;
he warms to the forks clinking against plates,
to voices rising and clashing at the dinner table,
where I would melt at the hum of a distant lawn mower,
as soothing to me in the country silence

as a lover typing in the other room.
How now more than ever, when my turn comes around,
I need him beside me, stirring the sauce,
or rubbing my back—reminding me why
I'm still here
cooking for fifteen people, all fire and cheer,
not alone with a book on Breezy Hill Road.

TRADITION

Oh how they love their kitchens
the women of Jerusalem
and their men, who grew up around
stoves, onions frying, eggplant
on the flame, peppers, tomatoes.
Around battered tables, spooning in
couscous with carrots and potatoes, or rice and
green beans, chicken soup, kubeh.
Around mothers bulging through flowered
dresses, kerchiefs on their heads,
happy to be cooking for their children

so that even here in Los Angeles
those children continue the tradition,
inviting friends to come like family
through the back door, to the grilling
and baking, center of the home.
They sit at counters in marble kitchens,
plates brimming with stuffed grape leaves
or hummus and salads, olives, pickles,
voices rising and bubbling with the steam
from the pots and the Middle Eastern melodies
on the stereo. And I,

who only adopted their city,
join in the feast,
savor salt and cilantro, lemon, cumin,
fill more and more with the glow. But still

I feel the pull of a different hearth,
the one I've known as center of the home,
where lamplight gleams on cherry wood
and talk flows softly from couch to couch.

RITUAL

Is it for our smiling faces
that she gets up at seven on Fridays to put an apron on
and stand in front of a hot stove, even in the summer heat
when the air conditioner is not working well, even when
her ankle is swollen and her medicine is making
her throat dry and her body tired?
Is it for the kisses planted on both her cheeks
that she cooks a feast every week for fifteen people?—
pot roast and carrots, chicken, salmon, eggplants,
and special vegetarian dishes for her oldest granddaughter.
Is it the ritual she loves?—setting wine and challah on a white cloth
so her children, some married, some with children of their own,
can come stand around her table and listen in silence
as one of her sons reads kiddush.
Or are these the gestures of a woman who gives without thinking?—
whose fingers turn a beet into a delicacy,
whose hands find pleasure in onions, parsley, and garlic cloves.

SPICE

It's the time of year I want to be there, not here:
back east, where the hills flush red as guilt,
as if a secret has been exposed.
But there is no secret; just October
in Vermont. Saffron, turmeric,
chili pepper on the leaves.

It's taken years for me to notice;
only now I can admit
that here, too, the trees break out
in spicy salsa flames—
though it's our winter that sizzles:
November and December
when liquid ambers blaze as brightly
as the maples I have yearned for.
Too long I've missed the scarlet
of crepe myrtles in L.A. . . .

not just leaves turning red,
not paprika, sweet or hot,
but the glow they spark in me—
and whatever in that fervor feels
like revelry, rebellion.
Something fierce unleashed
makes me blush like those hills.

CRAVING

Mid-September and I crave color,
red as Bloody Mary spilled on maple leaves;

want the wind to slam me back
into an orange mouth
with bright seductive tongues;

want the fever that lights up the sky
to light me up, too;
make me delirious enough
to sing *Libiamo* on the chairlift
to the top of Mt. Stowe—

though, afterwards, I'll have
nothing to show but

a handful of leaves
pressed like dried desire
between the pages of my book

and a paper bag full
of McIntoshes, so tart
they make me cry.

BURGERS AND PRAYERS

I am from quiet thrills, like snow padding
the hills, settling on pines and spruce,
swelling into drifts in the driveway—while icicles
hang and we, on flying saucers,
spin down towards the fence at the bottom.
From robins, corn on the cob, and apple
picking—McIntosh, tart on the tongue.
Books under blue skies, horizon humming,
and from time to time, puncturing the peace:
Ma, Steven's being a pest!

I am from noisy thrills, like pot roast
and Jewish rye bread in Bloomfield and Milburn
with Nana Ceil and Poppy Ben, Gussie—*Call me Grandma!*—
and Bill, paralyzed, watching sport on TV.
Cigarettes and scotch, and Harold asking—
through cigars—if the cat has got my tongue.

I'm from Vermont and New Jersey, Jerusalem, Los Angeles.
Part autumn leaves, part roses and stoops.
Part ancient prayer, part In-N-Out Burger.
What do I say when you ask where I'm from?
That I began in a basement, grew up in the fields?
That I crossed an ocean, then crossed it again?
Or that place doesn't matter, that I'm from
pimples and sunlamps, crushes, and dreams.

— After "Where I'm From" by George Ella Lyon —

LOVE IN THE TIME OF ALZHEIMER'S

We whisked away her high heels
when she began to trip on her vanity.
She wipes out the rest:
my sister's wedding,
ten great-grandchildren,
half a century of marriage
(Bill? A chemist, wasn't he?).
But she can still kiss in the elevator,
flirt with the orderly,
and eat her boiled chicken,
mashed potatoes, and jello
at a table set for two

because she's got her Moshe,
her bachelor friend:
his hand in hers
when I take her out for coffee
and pecan pie by the sea;
his lips brushing hers
after he photographs her by the fountain
near the pink marble Opera Building.

She left her other self blowing kisses
off the front stoop
in Bloomfield, New Jersey,
while her stories cook in the oven
with her mandelbread and pot roast,
but here, on Idelson Street, Tel Aviv—
around the corner from the pubs
where Romanian workers drink beer and
watch gulls flying low over the Mediterranean—
she stares at the unfamiliar city
trapped inside her window

and repeats herself, repeats herself,
tells me ten times
her teeth are like the stars:
they come out at night.

But, still, she's got *my Moishe*,

who leads her like a child to her lost bedroom
and waits for her to laugh
each time he removes the black beret
from his egg-bald head,

as I wait for her to say,
Your skin is so lovely, dear.

BLACK EYES

The black eyes of taxi drivers
follow me down the streets
of Jerusalem
where I get lost in smells
of pizza, shawarma,
fresh-baked cakes with names
like Mozart and Black Forest.

It is enough
to walk these streets again;
to drink a cold glass
of fresh-squeezed orange juice
from a corner stand
on Ben Yehuda Street,
where a soldier with an M-16
slung over his shoulder
downs carrot juice
in the mid-afternoon heat.

Strands of cigarette smoke
pull me forward
through narrow alleys
with white stone walls,
past the checkered heads
of Arabs in keffiyehs,
and the black coats of men
who flash by in droves
on their way to prayers.

If you were with me,
we'd buy peanuts for me
and sunflower seeds for you
to crack between your teeth
on the streets of your childhood.

You'd slip coins into the cup
of a one-legged beggar
who's sat on the same sidewalk spot
on Jaffa Street for thirty years.

I am alone this time,
but I drop five shekels
into the open case
of a Russian violinist

pouring *Polovtsian Dances*
onto the promenade.

The news is everywhere—
in the arms of the violinist,
in the black eyes of the city.
Another soldier killed
on the Lebanese border.

On a bench in a courtyard
you showed me once,
I eat falafel
and watch the sun light up
the kerchief of an old woman
peeling potatoes on a balcony.
Laundry flaps on clotheslines,
and from an open window
wails the black-eyed voice
of Boaz Sharabi on the radio.
Sometimes, it is enough
to be alive.

FIVE MINUTES

It was all a matter of silver rings
in the window of a jewelry shop
on Jaffa Street—
simplicity too beautiful to ignore—
so while I wasn't planning to buy a ring
that day, I went inside and tried them on,
starlight on tan fingers, again and again.
It was all a matter of the time it took
to choose the one with the lovely, turquoise stone
because if I had been faster, five minutes
faster, I'd have been right in the middle
of Zion Square when the bomb exploded.
Instead, I stepped back into the sunlit street
and saw a crowd surge towards me, screaming, bleeding—
my new ring shining like fate on my finger.

IN A ZIPLOC

The poet from Haifa rushes in, hand out
as though she's brought something special
for her editor in Tel Aviv.
Who is she? I wonder—
this gray-haired interruption
who's come from the war zone
and can't wait to share.
Look! she says.
Not a manuscript this time,
but a Ziploc full of scraps
she's collected from the street:
pieces of the rocket
that just missed her house.

I gather my poems, suddenly small,
while hers fills the room, insistent as the sirens
that wail in the North.
Loud as exploding Katyushas.
All there,
exposed on her palm:
raw, unpolished.

SURVIVAL

This could be about the gun
someone hides in a drawer
for self-defense
or about the duffel bag
I slip into our closet in Los Angeles,
bloated with earthquake supplies.

But I'm thinking about the boxes
I left in Israel
on the top shelf
of a metal cabinet
beside the washer and dryer:
a set of gas masks
for a family of five.

I am trying to remember
whether, amid the keys,
contracts, detailed instructions,
I told our new tenants
from England
anything about the black rubber masks
tucked away like memories of Scuds
descending on Tel Aviv.

And trying to understand
what makes foreigners
want to rent a house
in a country still packing
sealed brown boxes into its closets.

ON DOING NOTHING

Must be the hills that taught me to be still,
the long Vermont afternoons
spent lazing in a lawn chair,
cocooned from the world beyond.

Even here in Yael's humble yard
I'm content to ease out a blade of grass
and curl its coolness around my finger;
to gaze at this stretch of green
on the sands of Beer Sheva, at a few scattered
toys, broken or whole, and the fallen
white petals of the frangipani.

She—who grew up in this heat and dust
where there's always a basket of laundry to hang
and a floor to be washed; where the only
stable thing on the news is the weather—
she needs a cigarette
to make her stop running,
just sit and do nothing.

We laugh as she joins me for a rare intermission.
Later I will help with the folding, the clearing,
but, first, time-out on the grass.
I lean back, absorb, savor the moment.
She smokes and sips her Turkish coffee,
strong and bitter.

SWEET TEA

Dirt under his nails, cigarette
between his stubby fingers:
hands that know the feel of a cow's udder.
I watch those hands, my brother-in-law's,
busy now under bloated bellies,
fitting teats to the cups of milking machines.
Beyond him, in the Negev Desert, time is a camel
standing still under a hot sun, or a Bedouin
on his haunches, sipping sweet tea in his tent.
Over the black and white backs of cows,
I ask my brother-in-law, pacing in high rubber boots,
Wouldn't you like to be a Bedouin for a while?
My words drown in a sea of moos.
Bedouin? he shouts. *What?* He smiles, but doesn't stop.
He's got cows to usher in. Milk to deliver.

FOUR WOMEN FLOATING

I can't say why
why, at forty-six, it was such a thrill
sneaking into the kibbutz pool one night—
four women swimming laps under the moon,
the water still warm from the desert sun.
Breathing in, breathing out; just us
in the silence of orange trees and lemons,
potato fields fading into sand dunes and wadis,
acacias with long brown pods.
I can't say what made us spring,
weightless as ballerinas, across the pool,
bouncing off the balls of our feet,
gushing laughter into the soft dark air—
or why, as peacocks hurled cries of anguish
over the fence in the petting farm,
we lined up side by side,
holding the edge, pedaling with our legs,
and became four mothers merging
like sky into water,
sharing our stories,
letting go of our pain.

BREAKFAST ON THE BALCONY

Yes, I've come for ancient walls and olive trees,
violinists on cobbled streets, old stones
glowing pink in the late afternoon light—
but also for a lumpy sofa and a bowl of grapes,
medley of onions and laughter in stairways,
radios wailing through apartment walls.
And for this, my friend, just as it is:
your little balcony on the fourth floor
where a table stands among empty flowerpots,
broom, pails, boxes, and underpants
pinned to a clothesline with bras and towels—just right
when you dress it with sunflowers
printed on white cloth and bring out the tray
laid with napkins and silverware, yogurt,
fresh orange juice, coffee, toast and jam.
Lovely, sipping mugs while the sun shines
on TV antennas and geraniums,
rugs hanging over railings, and windows
holding the beginnings of stories.
What more could I ask for
than a chair at your bright yellow table,
high as clear skies, pine trees,
and the dusty red roofs of Jerusalem.

I FLY TO ISRAEL FOR MY MOTHER'S 84TH BIRTHDAY

We celebrate in the hills. My sisters spread blankets
on a grassy slope in the Forest of Angels,
Ya'ar Hamalakhim, and there, under pines and oaks—
our parents on beach chairs that seem to float away
in a sea of wildflowers—we feast on the lunch they've laid out
on a table in the clearing: lasagna and quiche,
schnitzel, potatoes, salads, fresh peppers.
No balloons at this party, but we have bright red
anemones, clusters of pink columbine, white-pink asphodel,
tangles of mustard weed, yellow and green,
and down below, in the valley, the woolly backs of sheep
that a Bedouin has brought to graze on the tall grass,
their *maaing* and *baaing* blending with the Arabic music
blaring from a radio nearby, where a group of men,
hands on each other's shoulders, bodies linked,
kick their legs, slide this way and that way,
marking the beat that echoes through the trees—
while we chat and laugh, our parents surrounded
by their children, grandchildren, great-grandchildren,
and I think: this is what I want, too,
a birthday party outdoors when I'm 84,
no walls around me, just a spot with a view,
sun warming my wrinkled cheek
while I gaze with pleasure at the family we've created
my husband at my side, details beginning to blur perhaps—
but what will that matter, if I can have a moment
of lasagna in the woods, cake and wildflowers and a birthday song
filled with the moaning of sheep and squeals of revelry
and, clear and emphatic, ever-present in my ears
my mother's voice, reminding me
once again that it's important to laugh,
at ourselves, our lives.

SPARKS

It could be an apple on an autumn day
or the branch it hangs from, or two apples,
one ripe, the other wrinkled and rotting—

though it's more about the one who
stands back for a moment, open
to whatever it is in that tangled tree
that awakens a spark.

Open to each jagged piece
and to the puzzle created;
the way it all fits together—

as it does one morning
on this Tel Aviv shore
where it's not just bikinis
and bright umbrellas and tongues
licking lemon popsicles,
but old folks with white caps on their heads,
bobbing on the waves or standing and chatting,
bellies protruding—and helicopters from time to time
suddenly intruding on this ordinary day,
rushing soldiers to the front
to fight for the lovely tanning bodies;
for the men on the rocks with their fishing poles
and the children making cakes and castles;
for the sand dripping through their fingers.

And, yes, for the young man
smoking his hookah on a blanket on the beach
as he stares into whirling propellers.

IN ISRAEL, TASTING KUMQUATS

Chinese orange, they call it in Israel.
Kumquat in English. My friend in Kfar Yedidiya
plucks some for me from the tree in her yard.
No, she says, when I begin to peel one
like a baby orange. *You eat the whole thing.*
I plop it in my mouth and fall in love
with its sweet rind, sour pulp. We hug,
say our good-byes. I leave richer,
a bag of kumquats on the car seat, treasured as gold coins.

Days later, I find them growing near the dining room
on Kibbutz Revivim, where I am visiting my family.
I pick some for my parents who also, somehow,
have never tasted them before, and they, too, delight
in these bright-colored balls. I eat them like candy, addicted
as I am to the guava in my sister's garden.
Lemons grow here. Olives. Feijoa.
Another friend gives me fresh-grown lettuce
from behind her home. And a cluster of green onions.

On my last day in this country, hours before my flight,
I hike with my sister and her family
among red kalaniot, anemones, in the Ben Shemen Forest,
smell of pines and grass, green after the rain.
We set a blanket down and have a picnic lunch
of schnitzel, baked potatoes, corn on the cob.
Here in the forest—where a man rests on a hammock
he has strung between trees and children laugh nearby—
we forget about stabbings, car rammings, shootings.
On our backs beneath a blue sky, we could believe almost anything.
We close our eyes. Peace feels real.

UPON RETURNING FROM A TRIP TO ISRAEL

How was your trip? they ask, puffing on cigarettes, stirring coffee,
poised at the other end of the telephone, more anxious, perhaps,
to share their news than to listen to mine.
It was good, is all I say,
good, meaning I lounged on a yellow beach chair,
seduced by the sun; frisked with friends in the waves
of the Mediterranean, laughing, always laughing—
on the same shore where a soldier, patrolling the Promenade,
sliced a garbage bag open to check for bombs.
Good, meaning the kissable cheeks of my nephew
as he bounced like a bright ball on the couch, behind my sister—
while we stared at the newspaper on the table,
at the remains of Sbarro Restaurant in Jerusalem, where a bomb
exploded, killing, among others, five members of a family
who drove into town that day for something as simple
as pizza and coke, and a break from war.
Good, meaning goose liver paté, fresh trout, desires stirred
by breezes at sunset on the balcony in Tel Aviv,
life going on amidst mortars and missiles,
drive-by shootings on the West Bank.
Good, I say, meaning yes, there's more,
but where do I start? And how?—when the story inside me
will only come out in the shape of a poem.

DO WE CALL THIS A FAMILY?

No, says my sister-in-law, stuck on what *was*,
on the bygones of of wine and challah . . .
because for years we were a table—
or two long tables joined in a T. Once a week
we were chicken and roast mixed with jokes and jabs
at the Sabbath meal, talking over each other
and into each other, loud in our zeal.
Afterwards, we were the chairs pushed back,
dishes cleared away; overstuffed bodies
sinking into sofas for tea and cake.
We were a bowl of nuts, an offering of fruit,
peeled and sliced and passed around.

But piece by piece, the table fell apart.
The lips that sipped the wine and blew out
smoke after dinner began to puff out sighs as well.
Some grew tired; others needed space. Or time
to nurse the mounting ills of mind and body,
pocket, bed; to tend to broken hearts.
Or perhaps we just evolved,
had our own growing tables.

Are we not still a family?—
one who gathered up the fragments
and carried them away, each to our own home,
like firewood in our arms, enough to keep us warm.
Or to store in our garages: treasures from past times.

The long table may be gone,
but we gather, we meet.
Are we not still the candles, the blessings
that grace a Sabbath meal?

TORAH IN THE FIELDS

Not you, but your question
has flown with me to Israel.

What makes it a Bar Mitzvah?
There's no rabbi, no synagogue, no Torah.
I see your point, Mother-in-law.
And now I also see poppies.
Yes, the poppies are out.
Mazal Tov! Mazal Tov! they call to my nephew
when we pass them on the trail in northern Galilee.
They are swaying, nodding,
deep in prayer and celebration.
Time to break out and bloom;
vibrant, red, they applaud *thirteen*.

The cows have come, too. Like rabbis,
they show us the way. They are everywhere:
on the hills, in the caves, the streams.
They leave warnings on the trail: where *not* to step.
This way, they say, higher and higher up the cliffs of Arbel,
and my nephew follows. The Kinneret shines below,
and in the water, his reflection: boy becoming man.

Later, in Ein Karem, we bless him in a garden
where grapes were once pressed into wine.
The steaks on the barbecue know this is a Bar Mitzvah.
They conspire with the stones in the courtyard,
the arches, the peeling walls, beautiful as frescoes;
with the lemons and the grapevine, the pink flowers of the redbud.
All of them whispering about the *mitzvahs* of this boy
whom we have gathered to honor
around a table bursting with fresh and tender and
sweet on a sunny day in Jerusalem.

YES, BUT—

There's always a *but*.
But is in the apples we choose in the market.
The Granny Smiths are good, we say . . . *but*
the Pink Ladies are better.
Tart as *but*, the Pink Ladies themselves
are probably thinking, in their own delicious way:
we respect our neighbors, the Granny Smiths, *but*
they are sour, green. Yes, they're apples like us, *but*
we don't believe them or trust them.
They roll over our borders, invade our space.
We would share it with them, *but*
they want it all for themselves.
We could compromise, maybe, with a Golden Delicious, *but*
we'll never make peace with a Granny Smith.

My mother-in-law blames me:
your fault, she says, that your children are assimilating.
But wants to argue and explain.
Call her intolerant. Defend their loves.
This time I just listen—eating the soup
she cooks every Friday. Sour and green.
Kubeh to die for. I take it in slowly,
can't get enough.

I begin to taste *and*.

And comes in gently; gathers all the apples:
reds, greens, yellows. It has no favorites.
Loves the Grannies *and* the Ladies.
Knows they all have some brown spots.
Doesn't make us choose.

WHEN I'M OLD AND DEMENTED

They say music helps. Old lips,
silent for years, begin to move again,
mouthing the words to a song once loved.

In the backyard, by the pool, we are listening to oldies
from the seventies. *Oh, baby, baby, it's a wild world.*
We look up, brightening: Cat Stevens singing *our* song.
Put that one on, I say, *when I'm no longer sure who you are.*
Maybe, as I lie in my nursing home bed,
it will carry me back to when I heard it playing
in a dorm on Mount Scopus where a window looked out
on olive trees and rock-studded hills; on the Old City down below,
its ancient stone walls turning pink in the setting sun.
I will hear those words, and it will all come back:
that dorm room in Jerusalem, two beds pushed together,
bedsprings squeaking beneath our love.

Let me hear *Hummingbird,* so I can sit on a bench
near my room in the Village, where Jaynie, my first Bahai friend,
taught me to use electric curlers and to pluck my eyebrows.
Put on *Bye, bye, American pie,* and I will dance again
in a high school gym in Springfield, Vermont,
and go parking with Ronnie on country roads.
I will feel his fingers unclasping my bra.

My friend tells me her mother recites Shakespeare,
but doesn't always recognize her family.
I won't be Juliet and you won't be Romeo,
but, please, if I stare at you vacantly,
hold my hand and whisper to me,
Oh, baby, baby, it's a wild world.

ACKNOWLEDGMENTS

These poems have been published in the following magazines or journals:

the Aurorean: "Yes, But—" and "Spice"
Bellowing Ark: "Burgers and Prayers"
Bloodroot Literary Magazine: "Survival"
Blue Unicorn: "Craving"
Coal City Review: "On Doing Nothing"
The Deronda Review: "Do We Call This a Family?"
The Ear: "In Israel, Tasting Kumquats"
Illya's Honey: "Tradition"
Jewish Affairs: "Once"
Jewish Journal: "Ritual"
Jewish Women's Literary Annual: "Sweet Tea"
Kulanu (Under One Canopy, Readings in Jewish Diversity, Edited by Karen Primack, Published by Kulanu): "Upon Returning From a Trip to Israel"
MacGuffin: "Black Eyes"
Mediphors: A Literary Journal of the Health Professions: "Love in the Time of Alzheimer's"
Moment: "Roots"
Nimrod: "In a Ziploc"
Pearl: "Five Minutes"
Poetica Magazine, Contemporary Jewish Writing and Art: "Where is Home?"
Quill and Parchment Magazine: "I Fly to Israel for My Mother's 84th Birthday" (second printing)
Social Justice Anthologies, a project of Beautiful Cadaver Project Pittsburgh, on theme, "Is it hot in here, or is it just me?": "When I'm Old and Demented"
Spillway: "Sweet Tea" (second printing)
Surprised by Joy, A Wising Up Press Anthology: "Breakfast on the Balcony"
The Times of Israel: "Torah in the Fields" (on The Blogs)
Wax Poetry and Art: "I Fly to Israel for My Mother's 84th Birthday"
Willow Review: "Four Women Floating"

Your Daily Poem: "Spice" (second printing)

"Ritual" was read on a program on BBC Radio 4 (September 11, 2016).
"Sparks" won Honorable Mention in the Anna Davidson Rosenberg Poetry Awards for poems on The Jewish experience (March, 2009).
"When I'm Old and Demented" placed as a Top 5 Finalist in *New Millennium Writings'* Monthly Muse Contest on the theme of music.
"Where is Home?" was performed by The Braid for their Salon Show on the theme, "Star-Spangled Sabra."

About the Author

Lori Levy's poems have appeared in *Rattle, Poet Lore, Nimrod International Journal, Paterson Literary Review, Poetry East,* and numerous other print and online literary journals in the U.S., the U.K., and Israel. Her work has also been published in medical humanities journals and in Jewish journals, including *Jewish Women's Literary Annual, Jewish Journal, European Judaism, Shirim,* and *The Reform Jewish Quarterly.* Her bilingual poetry book, *In the Mood for Orange,* was published in Israel in 2007, and her chapbook of color-related poems was published by Kelsay Books in September, 2023. Levy lives with her extended family in Los Angeles, but "home" has also been Vermont and Israel and, for several months, Panama while visiting her son and granddaughters.

The Jewish Poetry Project

jpoetry.us

Ben Yehuda Press

From the Coffee House of Jewish Dreamers: Poems of Wonder and Wandering and the Weekly Torah Portion by Isidore Century

"Isidore Century is a wonderful poet. His poems are funny, deeply observed, without pretension." – *The Jewish Week*

The House at the Center of the World: Poetic Midrash on Sacred Space by Abe Mezrich

"Direct and accessible, Mezrich's midrashic poems often tease profound meaning out of his chosen Torah texts. These poems remind us that our Creator is forgiving, that the spiritual and physical can inform one another, and that the supernatural can be carried into the everyday."
—Yehoshua November, author of *God's Optimism*

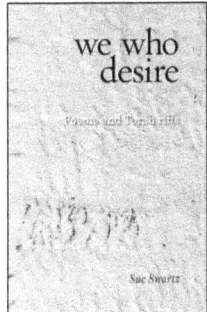

we who desire: Poems and Torah riffs by Sue Swartz

"Sue Swartz does magnificent acrobatics with the Torah. She takes the English that's become staid and boring, and adds something that's new and strange and exciting. These are poems that leave a taste in your mouth, and you walk away from them thinking, what did I just read? Oh, yeah. It's the Bible."
—Matthue Roth, author of *Yom Kippur A Go-Go*

Open My Lips: Prayers and Poems by Rachel Barenblat

"Barenblat's God is a personal God—one who lets her cry on His shoulder, and who rocks her like a colicky baby. These poems bridge the gap between the ineffable and the human. This collection will bring comfort to those with a religion of their own, as well as those seeking a relationship with some kind of higher power."
—Satya Robyn, author of *The Most Beautiful Thing*

Words for Blessing the World: Poems in Hebrew and English by Herbert J. Levine

"These writings express a profoundly earth-based theology in a language that is clear and comprehensible. These are works to study and learn from."
—Rodger Kamenetz, author of *The Jew in the Lotus*

Shiva Moon: Poems by Maxine Silverman

"The poems, deeply felt, are spare, spoken in a quiet but compelling voice, as if we were listening in to her inner life. This book is a precious record of the transformation saying Kaddish can bring."
—Howard Schwartz, author of *The Library of Dreams*

is: heretical Jewish blessings and poems by Yaakov Moshe (Jay Michaelson)

"Finally, Torah that speaks to and through the lives we are actually living: expanding the tent of holiness to embrace what has been cast out, elevating what has been kept down, advancing what has been held back, reveling in questions, revealing contradictions."
—Eden Pearlstein, aka eprhyme

Texts to the Holy: Poems
by Rachel Barenblat

"These poems are remarkable, radiating a love of God that is full bodied, innocent, raw, pulsating, hot, drunk. I can hardly fathom their faith but am grateful for the vistas they open. I will sit with them, and invite you to do the same."
—Merle Feld, author of *A Spiritual Life*

The Sabbath Bee: Love Songs to Shabbat
by Wilhelmina Gottschalk

"Torah, say our sages, has seventy faces. As these prose poems reveal, so too does Shabbat. Here we meet Shabbat as familiar housemate, as the child whose presence transforms a family, as a spreading tree, as an annoying friend who insists on being celebrated, as a woman, as a man, as a bee, as the ocean."
—Rachel Barenblat, author of *The Velveteen Rabbi's Haggadah*

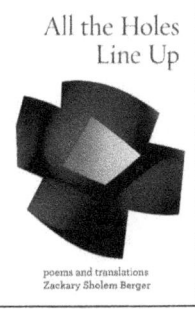

All the Holes Line Up: Poems and Translations
by Zackary Sholem Berger

"Spare and precise, Berger's poems gaze unflinchingly at—but also celebrate—human imperfection in its many forms. And what a delight that Berger also includes in this collection a handful of his resonant translations of some of the great Yiddish poets." —Yehoshua November, author of *God's Optimism* and *Two World Exist*

How to Bless the New Moon:
Songs of the Sovereign and the Icon
by Rachel Kann

"Rachel Kann is a master wordsmith. Her poems are rich in content, packed with life's wisdom and imbued with soul. May this collection of her work enable more of the world to enjoy her offerings."
—Sarah Yehudit Schneider, author of *You Are What You Hate* and *Kabbalistic Writings on the Nature of Masculine and Feminine*

Into My Garden
by David Caplan

"The beauty of Caplan's book is that it is not polemical. It does not set out to win an argument or ask you whether you've put your tefillin on today. These gentle poems invite the reader into one person's profound, ambiguous religious experience."
—*The Jewish Review of Books*

Between the Mountain and the Land is the Lesson: Poetic Midrash on Sacred Community
by Abe Mezrich

"Abe Mezrich cuts straight back to the roots of the Midrashic tradition, sermonizing as a poet, rather than idealogue. Best of all, Abe knows how to ask questions and avoid the obvious answers."
—Jake Marmer, author of *Jazz Talmud*

NOKADDISH: Poems in the Void
by Hanoch Guy Kaner

"A subversive, midrashic play with meanings—specifically Jewish meanings, and then the reversal and negation of these meanings."
—Robert G. Margolis

An Added Soul: Poems for a New Old Religion
by Herbert J. Levine

"These poems are remarkable, radiating a love of God that is full bodied, innocent, raw, pulsating, hot, drunk. I can hardly fathom their faith but am grateful for the vistas they open. I will sit with them, and invite you to do the same."
—Merle Feld, author of *A Spiritual Life*.

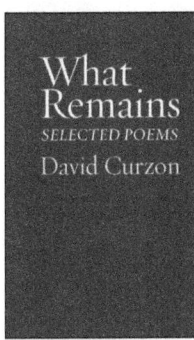

What Remains
by David Curzon

"Aphoristic, ekphrastic, and precise revelations animate WHAT REMAINS. In his stunning rewriting of Psalm 1 and other biblical passages, Curzon shows himself to be a fabricator, a collector, and an heir to the literature, arts, and wisdom traditions of the planet."
—Alicia Ostriker, author of *The Volcano and After*

The Shortest Skirt in Shul
by Sass Oron

"These poems exuberantly explore gender, Torah, the masks we wear, and the way our bodies (and the ways we wear them) at once threaten stable narratives, and offer the kind of liberation that saves our lives."
—Alicia Jo Rabins, author of *Divinity School*, composer of *Girls In Trouble*

Walking Triptychs
by Ilya Gutner

These are poems from when I walked about Shanghai and thought about the meaning of the Holocaust.

Book of Failed Salvation
by Julia Knobloch

"These beautiful poems express a tender longing for spiritual, physical, and emotional connection. They detail a life in movement—across distances, faith, love, and doubt."
—David Caplan, author of *Into My Garden*

Daily Blessings: Poems on Tractate Berakhot
by Hillel Broder

"Hillel Broder does not just write poetry about the Talmud; he also draws out the Talmud's poetry, finding lyricism amidst legality and re-setting the Talmud's rich images like precious gems in end-stopped lines of verse."
—Ilana Kurshan, author of *If All the Seas Were Ink*

The Missing Jew: Poems 1976-2022
by Rodger Kamenetz

"How does Rodger Kamenetz manage to have so singular a voice and at the same time precisely encapsulate the world view of an entire generation (also mine) of text-hungry American Jews born in the middle of the twentieth century?"
—Jacqueline Osherow, author of *Ultimatum from Paradise* and *My Lookalike at the Krishna Temple: Poems*

The Red Door: A dark fairy tale told in poems
by Shawn C. Harris

"THE RED DOOR, like its poet author Shawn C. Harris, transcends genres and identities. It is an exploration in crossing worlds. It brings together poetry and story telling, imagery and life events, spirit and body, the real and the fantastic, Jewish past and Jewish present, to spin one tale."
—Einat Wilf, author of *The War of Return*

The Matter of Families
by Robert H. Deluty

"Robert Deluty's career-spanning collection of New and Selected poems captures the essence of his work: the power of love, joy, and connection, all tied together with the poet's glorious sense of humor. This book is Deluty's masterpiece."
—Richard M. Berlin, M.D., author of *Freud on My Couch*

The Five Books of Limericks
by Rhonda Rosenheck

"A biblical commentary that is truly unique. Each chapter of the Torah is distilled into its own limerick, leading the reader to reconsider the meaning of the original text, and opening avenues for interpretation that are both fun and insightful."
—Rabbi Hillel Norry

Bits and Pieces
by Edward Pomerantz

"A stunning tapestry of family life in the 40s and 50s. Like all great poetry, Pomerantz's work expands after reading. Each poem is exquisitely structured, often with a stunning ending, into a masterful whole."
—Alan Ziegler, editor of *SHORT: An International Anthology*

Words for a Dazzling Firmament: Poems/Readings on Bereishit Through Shemot
by Abe Mezrich

"Mezrich is a cultivated craftsman— interpretively astute, sonically deliberate, and spiritually cunning."
—Zohar Atkins, author of *Nineveh*

Everything Thaws
by R. B. Lemberg

"Full of glacier-sharp truths, and moments revealed between words like bodies beneath melting permafrost. As it becomes increasingly plain how deeply our world is shaped by war and climate change and grief and anger, articulating that shape feels urgent and necessary and painful and healing."
—Ruthanna Emrys, author of *A Half-Built Garden*

Ode to the Dove
An illustrated, bilingual edition of a Yiddish poem by Abraham Sutzkever
Zackary Sholem Berger, translator
Liora Ostroff, Illustrator

"An elegant volume for lovers of poetry."
—Justin Cammy, translator of *Sutzkever, From the Vilna Ghetto to Nuremberg: Memoir and Testimony*

Poems for a Cartoon Mouse
by Andrew Burt

"Andrew Burt's poetry magnifies the vanishingly small line between danger and safety. This collection asks whether order is an illusion that veils chaos, or vice-versa, juxtaposing images from the Bible with animated films."
—Ari Shapiro, host of NPR's *All Things Considered*

Old Shul
by Pinny Bulman

"Nostalgia gives way to a tender theology, a softly chuckling illumination from within the heart of/as a beautiful, broken sanctuary, somehow both gritty and fragile, grimy and iridescent – not unlike faith itself."
—Jake Marmer, author of *Cosmic Diaspora*

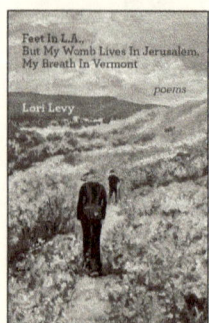

Feet In L.A., But My Womb Lives In Jerusalem, My Breath In Vermont
by Lori Levy

"Reading through Lori Levy's new book of poems takes my breath away. With no pretense whatsoever, they leap, alive, from the page until this reader felt as if she were living Levy's life. How does the author do it?"
—Mary Jo Balistreri, author of *Still*

www.ingramcontent.com/pod-product-compliance
Lightning Source LLC
Chambersburg PA
CBHW021028090426
42738CB00007B/941